The
GOLDEN AGE
of
STEAM

DEAN SERVER

SMITHMARK

This edition published in 1996 by
SMITHMARK Publishers, a division of U.S. Media Holdings, Inc.,
16 East 32nd Street, New York, NY 10016.

SMITHMARK books are available for bulk purchase for sales
promotion and premium use. For details write or call the
manager of special sales, SMITHMARK Publishers,
16 East 32nd Street, New York, NY 10016; (212) 532-6600.

This book was designed and produced by
Todtri Productions Limited
P.O. Box 572
New York, NY 10116-0572
FAX: (212) 279-1241

Printed and bound in Singapore

Library of Congress Catalog Card Number 96-68012
ISBN 0-7651-9778-2

Author: Dean Server

Publisher: Robert M. Tod
Editorial Director: Elizabeth Loonan
Designer and Art Director: Ron Pickless
Production Coordinator: Heather Weigel
Senior Editor: Edward Douglas
Project Editor: Cynthia Sternau
Assistant Editor: Shawna Kimber
Picture Researchers: Julie Dewitt, Natalie Goldstein,
  Kate Lewin, Cathy Stastny
Research Assistant: Laura Wyss
Typesetting and DTP: Blanc Verso/UK

PICTURE CREDITS

CONTENTS

INTRODUCTION 4

Chapter One
THE HISTORY OF STEAMBOATS 10

Chapter Two
A VARIETY OF STEAMBOATS 28

Chapter Three
THE HEYDAY OF THE STEAM LOCOMOTIVE 50

INDEX 80

ℐNTRODUCTION

The harnessing of steam power changed the world. Before the successful demonstration of Robert Fulton's steamboat in 1807, the ways mankind moved across land and sea were virtually unchanged for centuries. Transportation was dependent on natural elements, whether it was the wind in a boat's sails, a team of horses pulling a wagon, or a person's own two legs. The steamboat and the railroad opened a new world of possibilities to nineteenth-century society. People could travel farther with less effort and in much less time, and the opportunities for commerce and mass distribution of goods were enormous. In isolated wildernesses such as the American west, steam-powered transportation brought settlers and the supplies to sustain them. The availability and relative safety of the steamboats and railroads let far greater numbers of people travel and explore the world than had ever before been possible.

STEAM POWER ON LAND AND SEA

It was a tumultuous, fast-moving period in the history of transportation. Soon after Fulton's initial success, he and other entrepreneurs began to run commercial steamboats throughout the American waterways, including the Mississippi and the Great Lakes. In those early years, there were many technical problems with steamship travel, including numerous deadly fires. Nonetheless, the steamboat continued to expand its presence in the United States through the middle of the nineteenth century, and the rapid transportation on water it permitted also extended the horizons of American settlements.

The building of steamboats also progressed in Europe shortly after Fulton's success. Eventually, service was available on steamers running between England and most of western Europe. Soon,

Below: This quintessential 1866 Currier & Ives work entitled *Rounding The Bend* shows a trio of floating palaces heading down the Mississippi.

Ocean Cap.^{ne} Combes ainé

Above: A French steamer is the subject of this work by Antoine Roux entitled *Ocean Captain Combes the Elder*.

English steamers were also sailing to the outreaches of the British Empire, including Africa and India. French and Dutch steamers also reached distant ports, as the steamship proved itself much more capable of hauling large loads of freight than any of its predecessors. Passenger steamships were running regularly across the Atlantic Ocean by 1840. The transatlantic liners of Cunard and other companies continued to flourish through the rest of the nineteenth and well into the twentieth centuries, for the only competition these transatlantic steamers faced was from each other. The owners of these liners outdid each other building bigger, faster, and more elegant steam-powered vessels. Millions of Europeans immigrating to America also rode these ships, jammed into the much less glamorous third-class and steerage compartments.

The traveling engine, better known as the locomotive, achieved its earliest successes in England, beginning with George Stephenson's Stockton & Darlington Railway in 1825 and followed in 1830 by the Liverpool & Manchester Railway. Rail service came to London in 1836, and by 1840, British railroads were plentiful and prosperous. The other major countries of western Europe, particularly France and Germany, also constructed large railway systems by the middle of the nineteenth century. In America, the steam engine's use for travel over land was slower to reach prominence, for the success of the steamboat seemed to meet the needs of most travelers in the major cities as well as commercial traders. Another reason that the locomotive was slower to take prominence in early nineteenth-century America was that railroads were not only difficult to construct, they were also quite expensive. Between 1815 and 1825, several attempts to construct rail lines between major American cities

were unsuccessful due to insufficient funding.

By 1830, financing became more readily available in America for rail construction, and several railroad companies were founded. Late in 1830, the first passenger train in America passed through South Carolina, and the next year, regularly scheduled railroad service began. In the following few years, many more locomotives were built with increased power and speed, and a number of the routes which in the past had only been traversed by horse-drawn carriages were instead served by trains pulled by an "iron horse."

Between 1830 and 1850, American rail travel continued to expand significantly, connecting the largest eastern cities, most importantly, New York, Boston, and Philadelphia. As further advancements to the steam engine were made, the locomotive became powerful enough to replace the steamboat as a source for most commercial hauling. By the middle of the nineteenth century, favorable government legislation led to a great expansion of railroads in the American midwest. Rail lines were laid through the Great Lakes region all the way south to the Gulf of Mexico. The iron horse had thus become the dominant form of transportation throughout much of America. Its convenience, and particularly its speed, had made it more popular than the steamboat for business, commercial, and pleasure trips.

The success of the locomotive did not, however, mean the end of the steamboat. Though no longer the main source of public transportation, the steamboat became instead the center of leisurely and luxurious travel. Soon after the first steamboat sailed, owners of the vessels began attaching cabins to the backs of the boats. Originally, these cabins were decorated with curtains, carpeting, and other comforts, but in the ensuing decades, the

Above: Peter Cooper created the locomotive *Tom Thumb*, which became the first steam-engine in America to carry passengers. In 1830 it was challenged in a race with a horse-drawn rail car. Though the horse won that day, it was the locomotive that was the ultimate winner.

Overleaf: Locomotives at rest in the train yard sport powerful lamps and cowcatchers, essential for protecting train and passengers from loose livestock en route.

provisions for travelers became increasingly elaborate. Soon these boats were dubbed "floating palaces," and by the middle of the nineteenth century they were big enough to accommodate several hundred travelers. The furnishings became so lavish on some that costs ran as high as two million dollars. No possible ornamentation was left out, and no expense was spared. The ceilings were particularly elaborate, usually decorated in a Gothic or Norman style. In 1853, a writer in *Hunt's* magazine described one of the floating palaces as being "in a splendor of style that Cleopatra herself might envy." As the century progressed it became common for these boats to reach lengths of 300 feet (90 meters) and beyond, culminating in 1893 with the *Priscilla*, which sailed between New York and Boston. At 440 feet, (133 meters) the *Priscilla* was the longest steamboat built in the nineteenth century.

After 1908, no more floating palaces were produced. Railroads had advanced to a point where inland boat travel was no longer necessary. The construction of drawbridges over major waterways had made direct rail travel possible between major cities. Perhaps most importantly, rail travel had also become much more comfortable than it had been in its earliest days. No longer were floating palaces the only comfortable way to travel, as railroads added food, drink, and lodging to their services.

By the last decade of the century, the steam engine was also being surpassed. The invention of the diesel engine, which could operate on cheaper fuel, quickly became a popular source of power for both boats and locomotives after it was patented in 1892. The use of electric power for land travel began in 1895, with an overhead wire connected to the locomotive and a power line providing energy in large cities and in tunnels. As these cheaper and easier forms of energy took hold early in the twentieth century, the use of steam engines declined dramatically. Much as sailboats and horse-drawn coaches had been supplanted a century before, the success of diesel and electrical power meant that the Golden Age of Steam had ended.

Above: The sight of a shining clean train is now mostly taken for granted, but in the Golden Age of Steam, it was cause for much excitement.

Chapter One

THE HISTORY OF STEAMBOATS

Robert Fulton is credited with developing the first commercially successful steamboat, but his first American ship, the *North River of Clermont*, was not the first steam-powered vessel on water. Before Fulton, such inventors as Oliver Evans, James Rumsey, William Symington, and John Fitch had experimented with various seafaring uses of steam power late in the nineteenth century, though none had the success or financial backing which Fulton would have in 1807. Of the others, John Fitch was the most successful. As far back as 1787, a steamboat he constructed plied the Delaware River between Philadelphia and Burlington. The steam engines on this early vessel propelled the boat forward by raising and lowering a series of paddles; Fitch's subsequent boats improved on this technology with much more efficient paddle wheels.

Below: Robert Fulton (1765–1815) was not the first person to create a working steamboat, but with the backing of his wealthy benefactor, Robert Livingston, and his own entrepreneurial skills, he was the first to make the new technology a commercial success.

BEGINNINGS

By 1790, Fitch's steamboat, the *Thornton*, was operating commercially on the Delaware River, running at speeds up to 8 miles (12.8 kilometers) an hour, quite a bit faster than Fulton would reach in 1807. But though Fitch's ship ran regularly through the summer of 1790, it did not generate enough business to be successful. Not only were customers discouraged because of uncertainty about the safety of the trip, they also had access to stagecoaches—which could make the trip along the Delaware River faster. Fitch also ran up large debts while attempting to develop improvements for his vessels; in his remaining years he became impoverished and despondent after he lost his financing and could no longer continue his work. Though he had made great progress in advancing the use of the steamboat, Fitch committed suicide in 1798, with no money left and little recognition for his accomplishments.

Robert Fulton was not as innovative as Fitch, but he was a much more practical

Above: Fulton's original steamship, the *Clermont*, or as it was known in his lifetime, the *North River of Clermont*, made its initial trip up the Hudson River in 1807, traveling from New York City to Albany at three times the speed of other boats at that time. The *Clermont* remained in service until 1814.

businessman. With the help of a wealthy patron, Robert Livingston, Fulton was able to construct a steamboat which ran up the Hudson River in 1807. The engine he used was one he had bought from the successful Scottish engineer, James Watt. Unlike his predecessors, who had built their own engines, Fulton was not as concerned with originality as he was with creating something that would be both viable and practical. Utilizing his own knowledge of engineering along with the advancements developed by Fitch and others, Fulton designed a steamboat which made the trip from New York to Albany at a speed three times as fast as the boats which had been running the same route.

After the initial voyage, Fulton made several improvements to his boat. Accommodations for customers were installed, and he made sure the passengers' trip would be more pleasant by covering up the steam engine and its annoying noise. Soon the *North River of Clermont* began its commercial runs, which continued for seven more years until the ship was withdrawn from service in 1814. Fulton also built several other boats that continued to operate in and around New York State, realizing handsome profits for their owners. Fulton's entrepreneurial skills, coupled with Livingston's strong financial backing, turned the fledgling steamboat business into a thriving commercial success.

During the years following Fulton's first trip, other steamboats were built in surrounding eastern states. The first of these was the *Phoenix*, which was launched in 1808 in Hoboken, New Jersey, where it was built by John Stevens. But Fulton and Livingston had been granted a charter by New York State which gave them exclusive control of steamboat travel on the Hudson River for twenty years, and their monopoly denied the *Phoenix* and other steamboats access to the most profitable and heavily traveled eastern routes. Soon, the monopoly was challenged in court, though it was not settled until after both Fulton and Livingston had died. In 1824, the

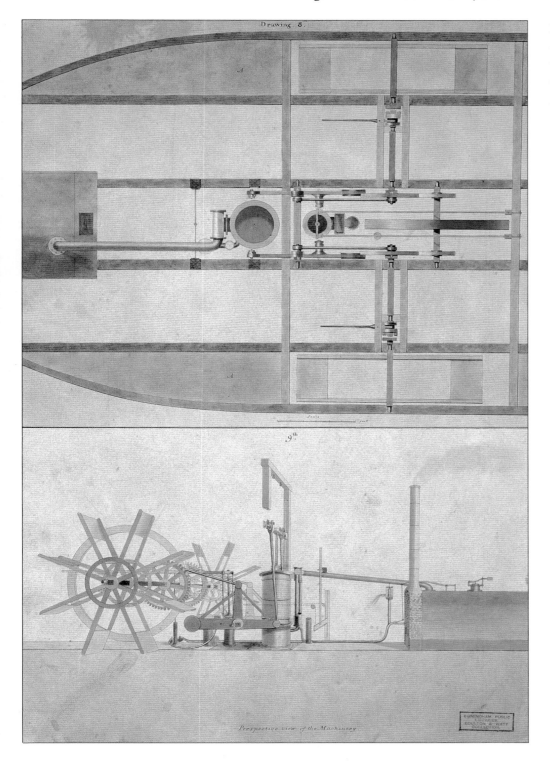

Left: After the successful runs of the *Clermont*, Fulton used these drawings of his hull and engine designs to apply for a patent in 1809.

Right: Ocean-sailing packets powered by steam began to appear in 1816 and became a common form of transportation between the major cities of Europe. Pictured here is one of those packets, the *Eagle*, shown here on her run from London to Margate in 1824.

Right: Early steamboat travel was not always smooth or safe, as the nineteenth-century engineers learned a great deal through trial and error. This cartoon from 1830 entitled "The New Way of Traveling by Steam" satirizes the dangers still prevalent at the time. Notice the name of the boat, the *High Flyer*.

The New way of Traveling by Steam !!

Below: This engraving depicts the journey of one of the earliest French steamers, the *Elise*, as it traveled between London and Paris in 1816—providing for travelers a "pleasing and continuous journey despite contrary winds and currents."

United States Supreme Court ruled the monopoly repugnant and thus invalid. American waterways were then open to all steamboat travel. In the east, as in the rest of the country, many more steamboats were soon built and in operation.

RIVER COMMUNITIES

A few years after the first successful commercial steamboat runs, another very significant development took place in America. The opening of the Erie Canal in 1825 linked the Hudson River with the Great Lakes and allowed manufacturing and agriculture to develop significantly in regions which had previously been too far away from the largest centers of population. The canal and the speed of the steamboats made it possible for farmers around the Great Lakes to reach the Hudson River and sell their goods and crops in the major eastern markets. The more convenient route and improved travel between the midwest and the east reduced cargo charges by as much as ninety percent.

After the opening of the Erie Canal, several major communities developed along the riversides of the Great Lakes–Hudson River trade route. Among these were Rochester, Buffalo, and Syracuse, all in western New York State. Another city which quickly expanded into a major center was Erie, the only Great Lakes port in the state of Pennsylvania. In Ohio, the greatest growth took place in Cleveland, which soon became the largest city in its state and a major center of commerce through its Lake Erie port.

Below: By 1835, steamships were a common sight on the rivers of England. In this engraving by H. Adlard, steamships and other vessels share the waters of the Thames at Gravesend.

Above: As the nineteenth century progressed, Europeans utilized the speed of the steamship to reach distant ports. This exotic work from 1859 shows the steamer *Ma Roberts* riding through the lower Zambezi as an elephant wades in the nearby shallow waters.

Right: The steamship's new supremacy in mid-nineteenth century ocean travel is depicted in this work entitled *Hail and Farewell*, in which a steamer, the *Leith*, passes a clipper ship.

Opposite top: Mail service between England and India was launched in 1842 by this steamer, the *Hindostan*, shown here as it departs from Southampton.

Besides the Erie Canal's great impact on business around the banks of the Hudson River and the Great Lakes, it also became the means by which much of the American midwest was settled. Soon after the canal was opened, steamboat owners made most of their money by moving huge numbers of European immigrants from the eastern cities they had landed in out to the open spaces of the midwest. Communities in Missouri, Illinois, and Iowa suddenly sprang to life with settlements of Irish and Scandinavian

Below: The layout and inner workings of a large-scale steamer from the mid-nineteenth century are detailed in this drawing from 1861. It was not until the beginning of the twentieth century that steamers ceased also to carry masts and sails.

HMS WARRIOR 1861

Above: Artist George Catlin's work, *St. Louis From the River Below,* depicts a large steamer on the Mississippi in the early 1830s.

Opposite: New Orleans' location on the Mississippi made it one of the world's busiest ports. Shown here is the city's crowded levee on Canal Street in 1900.

immigrants, among others. Wisconsin, with a particularly heavy influx of German immigrants, also grew rapidly.

MAJOR STEAMER LANDINGS

The most important steamer stop to be developed in the midwest was St. Louis. The area was first settled in 1764 by French fur traders, but it was not until 1817, when the first steamboat arrived, that it became a great river port. St. Louis' central location along the Mississippi River, as well as access to other major rivers such as the Ohio, soon made it the most important midwestern hub. The so-called "Gateway to the West" became the destination for all business from the east (which was going either west on the Colorado or south on the Mississippi), and the population grew by more than ten times in the twenty years following the first steamboat landing. Only New Orleans was a busier port in nineteenth-century America.

In the south, steamboats allowed for a large development of agriculture crops—in particular, cotton. In the first twenty years following the arrival of the first steamboat on the Mississippi River in 1811, the cotton belt of the southern states increased production by more than forty times. This was only possible because of the speed with which steamboats could bring the cotton crop to market. In the years before the Civil War, all the smaller streams and rivers of the south were loaded with smaller vessels bringing

Above: This Currier & Ives rendering of New Orleans' levee in 1884 shows a huge array of goods waiting to be shipped out, while nearby steamers fill the sky with smoke.

their loads of cotton to the big ports of the Mississippi. The most important of these ports was Memphis, Tennessee. Before 1819, Memphis was mostly undeveloped, but with its Mississippi River port, it soon blossomed into the biggest city in its state and a major center of industrial and agricultural products.

After the cotton arrived in Memphis or another upriver port, it would be shipped south to the base of the river and New Orleans—the destination for the millions of tons of cotton produced in the south annually—before being shipped by steamboat to northern markets. As the hub of this activity, New Orleans developed into one of the busiest ports of the world, but the era of prosperity ended with the city's defeat in 1862 during the Civil War.

EUROPEAN AND INTERNATIONAL PORTS

The steamboat industry grew rapidly in Europe, and steampacket transportation became available between the major cities. The steamboat also became of vital importance to European commerce because of its increased cargo-carrying capabilities. Steamboats could bring back goods produced in distant ports—in quantities never before available. Soon France, Holland, and especially England had steamboats sailing to the furthest points of their far-flung empires.

Following the initial successes of the steamboat on America's waters, the first attempt at transatlantic travel by steam was made in 1819. The *Savannah* traveled from the city of Savannah, Georgia to Liverpool,

England in twenty-seven days—powered by steam for approximately ten percent of the voyage. The trip was not profitable, however, and though several individual ships crossed the Atlantic from 1823 to 1838, no regular transatlantic service was attempted again for more than twenty years. In 1838, two British companies sent steamboats from Europe to America. Then in 1840, Samuel Cunard, a Canadian ship owner, began the first regular transatlantic steamer service with the *Britannia*, which sailed between Liverpool, England to Cunard's home province of Halifax before reaching its final destination—Boston. Among the passengers aboard the *Britannia* was a cow, which provided fresh milk to the other travelers. Cunard built many other steamships, and the passenger service across the Atlantic grew and prospered.

No American companies competed with the Cunard Line for nearly a decade. Then, in 1848, the Ocean Steam Navigation Company of New York began to run ships between America and Europe under a government contract to carry mail, but this service was discontinued after eight years. Also in 1848, the Black Ball Line inaugurated service between New York and Liverpool with a steamer called the *United States*, but this proved to be an unprofitable route and was discontinued within a year.

It was difficult for steamships to make continuous and efficient trips across the Atlantic. The long trip left a terrible strain on the machinery, but the biggest problem came from clogging caused by the salt from the saltwater used in operating the engines. Another major problem for the American ocean steamers was that they tried very hard to make their trips

Above: By 1840, the British navy used steam-powered frigates as part of their fighting forces. Here the *H.M.S. Terrible* is shown in combat in 1845.

y Franz Hanfstaengl

Left: The first steam-powered ship to cross the Atlantic was the *Savannah*, though it only utilized steam during about ten percent of the trip. The vessel is shown here as it arrived in Liverpool in 1819.

Overleaf top: The Collins Line was established in America in 1849 to rival Britain's Cunard Line in luxurious transatlantic steam travel. The first Collins ship, the *Atlantic*, is shown here in an 1850 lithograph by S. Walters.

Overleaf below: One of the earliest of the luxurious transatlantic steamers was the *Great Western*, shown here departing from Bristol for New York in 1838.

faster than their Cunard competition, which meant an extra effort was required from the machinery. The most intense rivalry with Cunard started in 1849 with the beginning of the Collins Line, which commenced service between New York and Liverpool. Collins ships had luxurious passenger accommodations, as well as carrying freight and U.S. mail. Although the transatlantic trip had been reduced to nine or ten days, the strain of making such a quick trip was not only tough on the machinery, it was also very expensive. Despite a large government subsidy and extensive commercial business, the Collins transatlantic steamers were not profitable. Just before the beginning of the American Civil War, during tough economic times, the government contract for the Collins ships to deliver mail across the Atlantic

was greatly reduced. Soon afterward, the company found itself in extreme debt, it then went out of business.

During the last half of the nineteenth century, American industries wanted greater access to the markets of Europe for their goods. In 1872, the Pennsylvania Railroad Company created the American Steamship Company, which began transatlantic steamer service between Philadelphia and Liverpool. The goal of the company was to increase its railroad business; freight sent on its railroads was then destined for its own steamers and thereafter sent on to the markets of Europe. The American Steamship Company ran successfully for over a decade before it was absorbed by an international corporation. The American trend to combine railroad interests with steamship lines climaxed soon after 1900 when American financier J. P. Morgan acquired controlling shares in Britain's White Star Line.

Above: Leisure travel by steam quickly became popular after Fulton's original success. Here is a large British yacht from 1819 known as the *London Engineer*.

Chapter Two
A Variety of Steamboats

Opposite: The opening of the Suez Canal in 1869 increased the importance of steamships, since sail-driven vessels had a very difficult time dealing with the fierce winds of the Middle East. This painting by Edouard Riou commemorated the voyage of France's Empress Eugenie for the canal's inauguration.

After their initial success in New York, Fulton and Livingston then tried to extend the steamship business to the vast expanses of the Mississippi River. In 1811, the Fulton-designed *New Orleans* became the first steamboat on the Mississippi, traveling from Pittsburgh to New Orleans. The ship was not properly designed, however, as its hull was not flat enough for the often shallow waters of the Mississippi. Miraculously, the *New Orleans* completed its journey despite flooding, earthquakes, sandbars, and attacks from local Chickasaw tribes.

STERN-WHEELERS AND OTHER INLAND BOATS

Other ship builders soon realized that the steamboats designed for deep waters would not do on the Mississippi River or other rivers with shallow

Below: In the late nineteenth century, the floating palaces of the Hudson River were more expensive and elaborate than their counterparts on the Mississippi. One of these was the *America*, shown here in an 1878 portrait by Antonio Jacobsen.

or obstructed waters. These required a flatter hull, one which would ride on the water, not in it as the ocean-going steamers did. They also needed more power than Fulton's design provided. The rivers running through the tropical climates of Florida, for example, could only be traversed by steamers with wheels on the stern, not on the side, otherwise the ships would not have enough power to work their way through the massive vegetation within the waters. Travel on the Missouri River also demanded stern-wheels, for boats going up that difficult river needed to withstand damage from falling trees,

rough currents, dangerous winds, and other obstacles.

Henry Shreve, a ship builder from Pennsylvania, constructed the steamboat which would become the prototype for future western steamers. Utilizing a higher-pressure engine which used less fuel and was easier to manage, Shreve's first steamboat, the *Washington*, had a flat hull, an engine which was centrally located, and extra decks added to make up for the space taken by the rearrangement of the engine. So efficient was Shreve's design that it made the upriver trip from New Orleans to Louisville in twenty-four days, a

voyage which had taken non-steam-powered vessels anywhere from four to six months. This proof of the superiority of the steamboat led to a quick growth of the industry in the west, and within forty years, more than eight hundred steamboats were operating on the Mississippi.

STEAM TUGBOATS

The expansion of American steamboat production after 1825 made most of the smaller steamers of the past obsolete. They did not have the size or cargo and passenger capacities of the newer steamboats, which were built to travel the longer routes opened up by the Erie Canal. The owners of these older steamers found other uses for them, however. The huge ocean-

Left: This 1894 Hudson River scene by Andrew Melrose is entitled *New York From New Jersey*. Some seventy years after the United States Supreme Court ended Fulton and Livingston's monopoly on steamboat travel, many different vessels plied the water on the river.

sailing packets which had started regular transatlantic service in 1816 weighed over 600 tons (540 metric tons) and usually required towing to be brought into shore. The older steamboats were able to perform this task and so their owners were able to keep them in use. Soon companies were formed which constructed steamboats specifically for use as tugs.

In the middle decades of the nineteenth century, the growth of this industry was rapid on both sides of the Atlantic, as English ship builders constructed a number of particularly large steam tugboats which labored in the major British ports. Soon, steam-powered towboats were made bigger, more powerful, and even faster. The earliest of these ships in England and America were all side-wheelers, but between 1850 and 1863, the propeller-

Providence and Stonington Steamship Cos Steamers,
MASSACHUSETTS AND RHODE ISLAND.
NEW YORK AND BOSTON VIA PROVIDENCE.
Daily from Pier 29 N.R.   Foot of Warren St. N.Y.

Above: In the last decades of the nineteenth century, the steamboats of the eastern United States became larger and more lavish. Among these was the *Massachusetts*, which traveled daily from New York to Providence and Boston in the 1870s.

Right: Steam tugboats were utilized to tow in the large clipper ships in use during the early and middle parts of the nineteenth century.

Opposite: This work by Olivia C. Starring places the steamboat *circa* 1889 amidst many other forms of transportation. It is entitled *Hudson River at West Point*.

Above: Steamboats were an important force during the American Civil War. These Federal steamboats are shown at Pittsburg Landing in Tennessee in 1862, the site of one of the war's bloodiest conflicts. One of the steamers was used by General Ulysses S. Grant as a headquarters.

driven tugboat became the industry standard. Its popularity was the result of the development of the "compound engine," which could operate on less fuel than any of the side-wheel tugs, making it more economically efficient.

The other main function of steam tugboats was to push large barges of cargo. The steamers constructed for this purpose were powerful stern-wheeled rafts which could move cargo of great size with unprecedented speed. Though called tugboats or towboats, the raft steamer functioned by nuzzling into the barge with its nose and pushing its load forward. The steam rafting industry flourished throughout most of the nineteenth century, even in competition with the rapidly growing railroad network. Eventually, diesel power replaced steam engines on tugboats, much as it did on most other forms of transportation.

EXTRAVAGANT OCEAN STEAMSHIPS

As transatlantic steamers became more common in the later years of the nineteenth century, ship builders and ship owners on both sides of the Atlantic tried to outdo each other in building faster ships with more luxurious accommodations. This was quite a change from the earliest days of ocean steaming. In 1842, Charles Dickens was quite unsatisfied with his cabin when he went to America on the original Cunard transatlantic

Above: The owners of rival steam-boat companies tried to outdo each other in luxury. The elegance and grandeur of the great floating palaces of the Mississippi are admirably depicted in this 1861 work by A. Persac.

Left: The dangers of high-pressured steam were always present in the early days of steamers—this was realized in 1840 with the terrible fire aboard the steamboat *Lexington*.

Above: Steamboat races became fairly common on the Mississippi, and some attracted great attention. Shown here is a midnight race on the river between the *Fulton* and the *Danna*.

steamer, the *Britannia*. He described his quarters as "a profoundly preposterous box," with a mattress as thin as "a surgical plaster." Conditions were much better by the end of the decade when the American Collins Line began to compete for business with the Cunard ships. The first Collins ship, the *Atlantic*, built in 1849, had 150 berths and two saloons, each between 60 and 70 feet long (18 to 22 meters). The *Atlantic* also included fancy painted glass and a well-decorated ladies' drawing room. The other ships of the Collins line, the *Pacific*, the *Arctic*, and the *Baltic*, were all built with similar extravagance.

Above: The artist James E. Buttersworth created this oil painting of the steam and sail ship *Western Metropolis.* By the early years of the twentieth century, steamship design had progressed to the point where masts with sails were no longer used.

Left: This stark 1865 Currier & Ives lithograph of the Civil War is called *The Mississippi in Time of War.*

Right: Steamboats required vast amounts of fuel and labor. Shown here is a typical scene of harsh labor aboard a nineteenth-century steamer.

Below The enormous liner, *The Great Eastern*, required several steam tugs to guide it to its berth after its launching in 1857.

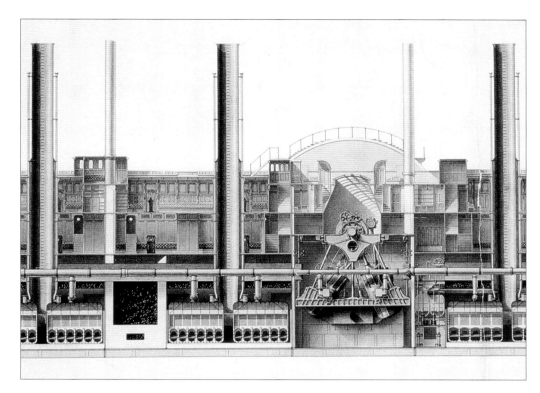

Left: This cross-section reveals the inner layout of the liner *The Great Eastern.*

Below: Steamships such as *The Great Eastern* were used for the laying of the transatlantic cable in 1865. In this drawing by R. Dudley, a buoy is lowered to mark the location of a break in the cable.

Above: The dangers faced by ocean liners from storms at sea were not always clear to travelers of the period. Shown here is a drawing from 1861 entitled *The Disaster of the Great Eastern: State of her Grand Saloon during the Gale.*

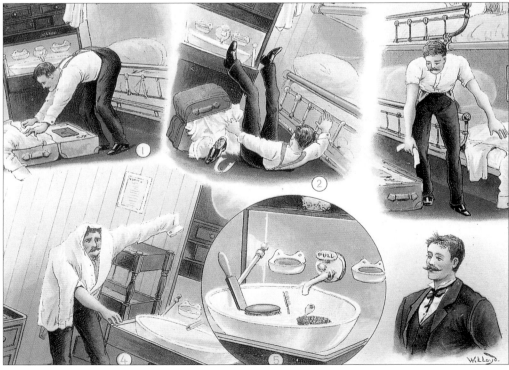

Right: Some of the problems posed by a wildly rocking boat before the invention of stabilizers are addressed in this series of drawings from 1890 by W. W. Lloyd called *Dressing For Dinner.*

In the later years of the nineteenth century, the ocean liners built in the United States did not have the glamour of those built in France or Great Britain. But nationalism played a role in transatlantic ship travel, as many Americans were happier to travel on an American ship, even if it offered fewer luxuries than the French and British lines. By 1891, the United States government had increased its subsidies for shipbuilding, and soon America had two of the fastest transatlantic steamers, the *St. Louis* and the *St. Paul*, both made totally of American materials.

In the early years of the twentieth century, the dominant shipbuilding nations sailing the Atlantic were Germany and England. Ocean steamship design had progressed to where masts were no longer used on board, wooden paddle wheels had been replaced by far more efficient screw propellers, and condensers produced fresh water for the engine rather than the troublesome salt water previously used. The big ships built just before World War I, including the ill-fated *Lusitania* and *Titanic*, emitted the smoke from their vast engines from four giant funnels.

THE FLOATING PALACES

In the last half of the nineteenth century, much as ocean transatlantic steamers were trying to outdo each other in luxurious accommodations, so, too, were the owners of the steamboats which sailed the rivers of America.

Above: This cutaway section of the interior of a large ocean liner shows how the vessel remained stabilized even on stormy seas.

Overleaf: The nineteenth-century luxury liner *S. S. America* steams ahead in all its glory.

Many of the most famous of these so-called "floating palaces" plied the Mississippi River, though the luxury boats of the eastern rivers were often just as fancy and usually more costly. As was also true of the ocean liners, travel on a floating palace became a favorite activity of the rich, and for corporations or the super-wealthy, owning a floating palace was the ultimate status symbol.

One of the first of the floating palaces was the *Eclipse*, with its 300-foot-long (91-meter) saloon and stained glass skyline, which rode the Mississippi starting in 1852. In 1861, the most famous eastern steamer of the era was launched, the *Mary Powell*. Like the *Eclipse*, the *Mary Powell* was also 300 feet long (91 meters), but unlike the *Eclipse* or almost any other floating palace, she did not have a bar, nor did she have gaudy decorations and facilities. What she did have was elegant simplicity and speed; the *Mary Powell* was the fastest boat on the Hudson River for more than twenty years.

Among the first of the floating palaces which ran on the Mississippi after the Civil War was the *Grand Republic*. She was launched in 1867 and used St. Louis as her home base. She cost $365,000, a price tag made larger by her oil-lamp chandeliers and Brussels carpeting. The *Grand Republic* was one of the most expensive boats on the Mississippi in those years, but other steamers in use at the time also offered every possible convenience to lure

Above: The fine architectural details of late nineteenth-century steamships is apparent in this photo of the lounge of the British liner *Empress of Britain*, dating from about 1885.

Opposite: Germany constructed some of the biggest and most luxurious ocean liners in the late nineteenth and early twentieth centuries. This photo from 1900 of the *Deutschland* shows part of the ship's massive dining room and lavish decorations.

customers. The *Richmond*, which had served in the Civil War before becoming a floating palace, published a daily newspaper for its riders, and also had its own on-board band and orchestra. Another ship with even more to offer was the *J. M. White*. Launched in 1878, it was 320 feet long (97 meters), cost $300,000, and had a capacity of 350 passengers—who were served dinner on specially designed china, completed with monogrammed linen and silverware. The furnishings of the *J. M. White* could not have been any more elaborate, with Brussels carpeting and furniture imported from France. The boat developed a huge reputation on the Mississippi, but it fell victim to a fire in 1886, just eight years after its first voyage.

Since the beginning of steamship travel and actually long before, it was quite common for boats to race. The title of fastest boat on a particular route was not only prestigious but often commercially significant. One of the greatest races during the era of steamship travel was in 1870, between two of the most famous floating palaces of the time, the *Natchez* and the *Robert E. Lee*. The race was from New Orleans to St. Louis, covering a total of 1,200 miles (1,932 kilometers), and drew international attention. The major cities of the United States as well as Europe all took notice of the event, and in all locations there was a great deal of gambling on the outcome. With most of the population of New Orleans turning out to see

Below: Two steamships from England's naval forces—the *Sovereign* and the *Destroyer*—are captured in this work by H. Monjo.

the start of the contest at the city's levee, businesses suspended operations, and schools closed all along the route for people to get a glimpse of the two competing steamers. The race itself did not measure up to its notoriety, however, with the *Robert E. Lee* gradually pulling away from the *Natchez* and reaching St. Louis about four hours ahead of its rival.

Late in the nineteenth century, the most expensive of all floating palaces were constructed in the east and ran on Long Island Sound. The three most famous of these were the *Pilgrim*, built in 1883, the *Puritan*, from 1889, and the *Priscilla*, from 1893. Each of these ships was bigger and better than the one that preceded it. The elite from all over the world came to Long Island just to ride these lavish steamers. The *Pilgrim* was 390 feet long (118 meters) and could hold over 1,200 passengers. The *Priscilla* was 440 feet long (133 meters) and held over 1,500 passengers. No expense was spared, and the cost of the *Priscilla* was $1,500,000.

After the *Priscilla*, the era of the floating palaces drew near to an end. Trains, which were much faster, soon took away most of the transportation business from America's river steamers both in the east and west. In 1908, one last floating palace was built to run on Long Island Sound: The *Commonwealth* was longer, more expensive, and even more elaborate than the *Priscilla*. But she was the last of her kind.

Below: By the time of the Spanish-American War in 1898 the world's navies had converted from sail to steam. Here, a line of American warships leads the attack in the Battle of Santiago, Cuba.

Chapter Three

THE HEYDAY OF THE STEAM LOCOMOTIVE

Opposite: Construction of tunnels was a laborious process on all railroads. Shown here is work from 1837 on the Kilsby Tunnel of the London & Birmingham Railway. Overhead is a working shaft for ventilation.

*M*uch the same way that Robert Fulton is credited as the originator of steamboat travel (although others had preceded him), so is George Stephenson held as the inventor and founder of the railroad—though he did not create the first steam-powered land vehicle nor was he the first to run a locomotive over rails. Nicholas Cugnot had built a steam-powered tractor in France as early as 1769, and Scotland's William Murdoch devised a steam tricycle in 1784. The first self-propelled vehicle to run over land in America was invented in 1804 by Oliver Evans. It was an amphibious vehicle he called "Oructor Amphibolis." A major breakthrough also occurred in 1804 in southern Wales, where the Cornish engineer Richard Trevithick built a steam-powered engine which hauled a load of 9 to 10 tons (8 to 9 metric tons). In the next twenty years, such inventors as John Blenkinsop, Matthew Murray, William Hedley, and William Brunton all devised engines which made successful runs on rails, though they had little speed and carried no passengers.

Above: Steam locomotives became more efficient as the nineteenth century progressed. This diagram shows the more centralized location of the power source behind the first wheel.

BEGINNINGS

In 1825, George Stephenson and his son Robert supervised the creation of the world's first locomotive passenger railway in the English county of Durham. Though no such railway had ever before existed, Stephenson convinced the financiers of the enterprise that his locomotive would be a more effective means of transportation than the proven and reliable horse. Much as Robert Fulton had used his entrepreneurial skills to aid in the

Right: At first, early in the nineteenth century, locomotive engines were developed to make it much easier to transport heavy materials such as coal. The idea of transporting people came later.

Below: This illustration (prior to 1830) of a railway steam engine called *Locomotion* shows a clean and shining locomotive, untouched by coal dust or flying soot.

acceptance of the steamboat, Stephenson had to be more than a brilliant engineer. He was considered to be a superb organizer and an excellent public speaker, and he utilized those and other skills to be appointed chief engineer of the railway in Durham, where he oversaw the construction of the 20 miles (32 kilometers) of rail lines between the towns of Darlington and Stockton.

The engine created by the Stephensons for this first passenger railway was known as *Locomotion Number 1*. On its initial run, it carried 450 passengers and hauled a total of about 30 tons (27 metric tons). It traveled at an average of about 8 miles (13 kilometers) an hour, reaching speeds as high as 12 miles (19 kilometers) an hour. In 1829, the Stephensons gained the assignment for an even bigger project, the construction of a new Liverpool & Manchester Railroad. The locomotive designed by Robert Stephenson to run on this new line was called the *Rocket*. It was more reliable and easier to operate than the other engines of the time, and it was about twice as fast as the locomotive used on the Darlington & Stockton Railway.

After their two major successes, the Stephensons became the dominant force in locomotive construction, and their accomplishments did not go unnoticed in America. The Delaware and Hudson Canal Company ordered three locomotives from the Stephensons for the purpose of hauling coal in Pennsylvania from the mines of Carbondale to the site of the company's canal construction in Honesdale. Only one of these was ever used, the

Above: Robert Stephenson's famous British locomotive of 1830, the *Rocket*, won a competition in Merseyside because of its dependability and efficiency. The *Rocket* continued to operate for more than a decade.

Above: The continued expansion of rail travel required new rail lines to be constructed, as in this view of England's Seven Oaks Tunnel, shown undergoing expansion in 1868.

Stourbridge Lion, the first locomotive to run on a commercial road in the United States. In 1829, with only a young engineer named Horatio Allen aboard, the *Stourbridge Lion* made its first run on tracks built the previous summer. But at 7 tons (6.3 metric tons), more than double the size the canal builders had expected, the *Stourbridge Lion* was too heavy for the tracks she ran on, and after only two runs, the engine was quickly withdrawn from service.

The *Stourbridge Lion* was the first true steam locomotive to run on rails in the United States, though a miniature engine and track had been built in 1825 by John Stevens of New Jersey. In 1830, New York philanthropist and engineer Peter Cooper created *Tom Thumb*, a locomotive which became the first steam engine in America to carry passengers. Reaching speeds of 18 miles (about 29 kilometers) an hour, the *Tom Thumb* hauled a carriage of twenty-six people which traveled 13 miles (21 kilometers) from Baltimore, Maryland, to the town of Endicott Mills. The success of this run convinced the Baltimore & Ohio Railroad to abandon horse-drawn carriages in favor of steam locomotives, a decision that made the Baltimore & Ohio one of the major forces in American transportation.

After Horatio Allen's work with the Delaware and Hudson Canal Company, he soon found a more important assignment—chief engineer of the South Carolina Railroad—and in that position, he ordered the purchase of several steam locomotives. The first to operate was called the *Best Friend of Charleston*, which, in 1831, became the first commercially

Left: Some of the earliest trains appeared to be a series of linked stagecoaches, as can be seen in this 1831 lithograph of the Liverpool and Manchester Railway which shows a train passing under the Rainhill Bridge.

Left: George Stephenson was in charge of the construction of the first major British railway, the Darlington & Stockton. The festive occasion of its opening in 1825 is recorded in this oil painting by Terence Cuneo.

Overleaf top: Here, a train passes through a tunnel during the early days of English railroading. The spread of rail systems across the countryside caused the development of new engineering and construction techniques.

Overleaf below: British monarchs were riding trains soon after their advent in England, as is evident in this 1844 portrayal of Queen Victoria disembarking from the royal train.

successful locomotive in America. It was also the first American engine to haul a train. On its first commercial trip, it carried three cars and approximately fifty passengers while traveling at speeds over 20 miles (32 kilometers) an hour.

After the success of the *Best Friend of Charleston*, many other eastern states soon began to operate railways, including Pennsylvania, New Jersey, and New York. The superior speed of the locomotive soon gave it an edge over

Right: Queen Victoria, Prince Albert, and some of their children are shown in this lithograph from the 1840s, which takes a look inside the royal railroad carriage.

Below: The bustling and colorful nature of a nineteenth-century English railway station is evident in this 1862 painting by William Powell Frith.

the steamboat in passenger traffic, though it could not yet match the freight-carrying capabilities of the sea-going vessels. The number of rail lines expanded quickly in America, reaching 3,328 miles (5,358 kilometers) in 1840, a number which would increase almost ten-fold in the following twenty years. Railway production developed in other countries as well. Canada's first rail service was built in 1836. In Europe, Germany, Italy, and the Netherlands also built their first rail lines during the 1830s. In Great Britain, there were 1,500 miles (2,415 kilometers) of rails by 1840, a total which had increased by more than five times by 1860. Some British colonies also were quick to develop rail lines, particularly India, which by 1900 had 25,000 miles (40,250 kilometers) of rails.

PROGRESS AND CORRUPTION

One major problem in the development of the American railroad industry was the so-called "robber barons"—financiers who invested in railroads and used every possible trick to swindle both the public and the government. One of the most legendary robber barons was Thomas Durant of the Union Pacific Railroad, who altered surveys to unlawfully increase government grants, manipulated new rail routes to maximize profits, and helped to create a fraudulent company which illegally received large government contracts. This last act led to one of the largest government scandals in United States history.

The managers of the Union Pacific's western competitor, the Central Pacific Railroad, also created their own "dummy" construction corporation which produced a profit of more than sixty million dollars. Yet another large scale

Above: The Erie Railroad was one of the busiest in America in the nineteenth century. This Currier & Ives lithograph from 1876 shows trains departing from the crowded Erie Station in Hornellsville, New York.

Opposite top: An early twentieth-century view of England's busy York Station, showing trains waiting to depart.

Opposite below: The speed of the locomotive changed the parameters of American life. The title of this 1863 Currier & Ives lithograph describes these two sleek locomotives as *The Lightning Express Trains.*

Right: The importance of the locomotive increased as the nineteenth century progressed, and it took over much of the business of the steamboat. Notice the prominence of the express train in this 1864 painting, compared to the distant steamboat.

scandal involved the Erie Railroad. Such noted financiers as Cornelius Vanderbilt, Jay Gould, Daniel Drew, and Jim Fisk all schemed to drain as much money as possible from the company (and stockholders). After various speculations, stock manipulations, and leverage deals, the Erie Railroad was almost seventy million dollars in debt and a much weaker company.

Somehow, despite these and other scandals, the railroad industry in America continued to prosper and expand. From 1850 to 1860, the total mileage of rail lines in the United States more than tripled. An example of the rapid growth can be seen in Ohio and Illinois. Neither state had many rail miles in the 1830s, but by 1860, they were first and second in the country in that field. Steam engines were also becoming more powerful. Coal had replaced wood as the main source of fuel, and this allowed locomotives to carry much heavier freight than in the past, greatly expanding that part of the railroad industry. In the 1870s, another major advance took place when rail sizes became standardized throughout America. This helped to further the unification of all American railroads and came close to linking all the major lines.

RAILROAD STATIONS

As trains became increasingly significant in the nineteenth century, the train station or depot became the most important location in every town. Not only was it the place where travel began or finished, but it was also the center of commerce where all commercial goods arrived, and so grain elevators, coal and lumberyards, and facilities and services for livestock were constructed adjacent to many depots. The station was also the place where all contact with the outside world was made; telegraph messages were sent or received and all mail and newspapers arrived there for distribution.

Originally, there were no train stations, just designated locations in a town where the train would stop. When actual depots were first built, they were usually little more than wooden sheds. Later, a standard design for smaller towns was devised. These usually included a ticket office, a baggage room, a waiting room, and facilities for men and women. In many smaller towns, there was one agent at the railroad station who handled all assignments. He sold tickets, handled baggage, operated the telegraph and the mail service, and often was also responsible for the control of train traffic.

Right: Circuses were among the early commercial users of the railroad. The freight-carrying capabilities of the locomotive allowed for long-distance transportation of large animals, as shown in this poster for the gigantic Robbins Brothers Circus.

Above: The construction of the railroad through the American West took, as hinted at in this picture, many years and an amazing amount of manpower.

Opposite top: The historic connection of the transcontinental railroad took place in Utah in 1869. Here, representatives of the Union Pacific and Central Pacific Railroads join hands to mark the occasion, and mark the spot by driving in a golden spike.

Opposite below: The process of creating and laying track for the first transcontinental railroad in the United States was a huge project, but America's virgin forests had ample timber to supply the vast number of railroad ties required.

Construction of large scale stations in the major cities developed quickly in the 1840s in both Europe and America. London's Waterloo Station was constructed in 1844. In 1848, the Union Depot of Providence, Rhode Island, was finished to much acclaim, and praise was also offered for New Haven's Union Station, which opened in 1849. Soon, large stations were also constructed in other major eastern cities, including New York, Baltimore, and Philadelphia. Most of these new, grand edifices had large entrances, very high ceilings, immense waiting rooms, and a very prominent clock. Many of them also had large Immigrants' Rooms, for the millions of Europeans who arrived in New York during the last half of the nineteenth and early twentieth centuries were then sent to various railroad lines, which took them to their final destinations.

When railroad stations were built in the big cities, more attention was given to architecture. A variety of architectural styles was employed, and the Romanesque style was one of the most popular designs of the time, thanks to the influence of American architect Henry Hobson Richardson. The Park Square Station in Boston, which opened in 1872, was built in a Gothic style. Some of the great stations built in the west, including Los Angeles' La Grande Station of 1893, were constructed in a Moorish design. There was also a particular style of station built in Canada, known as "Canadian Pacific," after the railroad which owned the stations. Using the designs of American architect Bruce Price, these structures, including Montreal's Windsor Station (1888), had features which were reminiscent of the grand castles of France.

Right: By the turn of the century, the interiors of railway passenger cars were both elaborate and comfortable.

Previous page: Edward Lamson Henry's 1867 portrayal of a busy train depot is entitled *The 9:45 Accommodation.* As was common at the time, the horse-driven carriages provided transportation to and from the station.

INTO THE WILDERNESS

The advent of railroad travel with its high speed and dependability brought a great deal of added convenience in Europe, and several international train lines were soon developed. One of the most famous of these is the *Orient Express*, which was inaugurated in 1883. Renowned for its superb accommodations and its elegant service, the line began in Paris, then stopped in Strasbourg, Munich, Vienna, Budapest, and Bucharest before reaching its final destination in Istanbul (then still known as Constantinople). During the first six years, the final passage between Bucharest and Constantinople was made by water on a steamer, but by 1889, the entire trip was made by rail.

During the same era, major railroads were also built across Asia. One of these was the Trans-Caspian, also known as the Central Asiatic. It began at Krasnovodsk on the Caspian Sea, and ended at Samara on the Volga. The most mammoth of the Asian railroads built in the late nineteenth century was the Trans-Siberian Railroad, which was over 4,000 miles long (6,440 kilometers) and was completed in 1905 after thirteen years of work. It linked European Russia with the Pacific coast port of Vladivostok.

NEW ROUTES AND LANDS

The arrival of the locomotive made travel much easier in Europe, but it did much more than that in Asia and North America. The Trans-Siberian Railroad allowed for large-scale colonization of Siberia for the first time, and

Right: The observation car of the Presidential train, with President Benjamin Harrison seated on the right.

Below: This cozy family scene aboard an English train of the 1850s demonstrates the increased comfort of rail travel that had developed in a short time.

Right: Writers and other artists discovered that the exotic locale of a train added an element of mystery and intrigue to a drama, such as this murder portrayed in a French work from 1901.

within a few decades the population of that region had doubled. In North America, the effect of the locomotive was even more dramatic. It created the opportunity for travel into areas previously unreachable, and allowed the western half of the continent to be settled much faster than anyone had anticipated.

Railroad expansion developed rapidly after the Civil War. The first transcontinental railroad had already been discussed for many years when President Lincoln signed the Pacific Railroad Act into law in 1862. This act provided grants and loans of federal aid which helped make construction of the transcontinental route economically feasible for the railroads. The two companies who undertook the monumental task were the Central Pacific,

Left: Train robberies were not just a problem in America's Wild West but in Europe as well. Here, three French bandits are shown robbing a train in 1907.

Below: The horror of a train accident offered a dramatic subject for many artists, including the anonymous painter who detailed this wreck in France in 1842.

Right: As railroads went further into the wilderness, engineers could expect to encounter unexpected obstacles on the tracks, such as an elephant, shown here in Siam in 1908.

UN ÉTRANGE ACCIDENT DE CHEMIN DE FER AU SIAM
La locomotive heurte un éléphant dans la nuit

Opposite top: The inspirational sight of a sleek locomotive moving through the countryside is shown in this painting called *Midland Railway Morning Scotch Express*.

Opposite below: A fast-moving locomotive makes its way through the snow-covered countryside. Travel at all hours of the day or night as well as in all seasons was one of the many advantages of railroads.

which worked its way east from California, and the Union Pacific, which went west from Omaha, Nebraska. Work on the railroad went on for years, and had to overcome a multitude of problems, including attacks by wild animals, severe weather conditions, mountainous terrain, and raids from Native Americans, primarily from among the Sioux Tribes. Tens of thousands of laborers toiled on the job, many of whom were immigrants. The Central Pacific found that they got very reliable work from the multitude of Chinese who had settled in California, and at one point, up to

90 percent of their laborers were Chinese. Much of the Union Pacific's work force was made up of Civil War veterans. The work of the two great railroads was finally completed in 1869, when their lines met near the great Salt Lake at what was called Promontory Point, in what was then the Territory of Utah.

Similar expansion of rail lines occurred in Canada. After its first railways began running in 1836, Canada started year-round service in 1851. By 1880, the country had more than 7,000 miles (11,270 kilometers) of rails, most of them near the country's southern border and well integrated with the United States' network. By 1885, the Canadian Pacific Railroad had constructed a line past the Rocky Mountains and had reached all the way across the country. It was then possible to ride a single train all the way across Canada.

RAILROAD TOWNS

Much as the steamboat virtually created new American cities such as St. Louis, New Orleans, and Memphis, the coming of the railroad also meant the large expansion of certain locations. The largest city that owes its prominence to the railroad is Chicago, Illinois. In 1830, before the railroad arrived, the total population of the location which was to become the city of Chicago was only about forty people. But after the locomotive started to travel through the area beginning in 1848, the city grew dramatically. From 1850 to 1860, Chicago's population rose from about 29,000 to well over 100,000, and, by the last half of the nineteenth century, the city had become America's main shipping center for all rail traffic. Several major

Above: The timeless romantic image of rail travel still has wide appeal today, as shown here in a modern photograph of a train silhouetted against the setting sun.

Opposite top: With an unusual connection of three engines, a train surges across the great distances of the wide prairies.

Opposite below: The *Reading Doubleheader* has two engines attached to the front to provide greater power. Such an arrangement was necessary when pulling long, heavy loads or when moving through steep terrain.

Opposite: The completion of many trestle bridges, such as the one seen here, made direct service between the major American cities possible, cutting transit time considerably.

Left: Railroad lines continued to expand well into the twentieth century, reaching out in all directions, and cities such as Chicago grew as the American rail hubs matured.

Below: The *Orient Express* connected major cities throughout Europe and became legendary for its excitement and romance. Here a French theater has produced a poster to look like an *Orient Express* advertisement.

railroads went through it, including the Chicago and Northwestern, Illinois Central, and Michigan Central. In fact, there was so much train travel in and out of Chicago that, beginning in 1885, six large train stations were built in the city over a forty-year-period, more than anywhere else in the country.

Further west of Chicago, another major rail hub developed in Omaha, Nebraska. The arrival of the railroad allowed that city to become a major center for both agriculture and livestock. The railroad brought in products that were used to develop these industries, and then shipped out what was produced to other markets. The city grew dramatically in the years following the construction of the city's railroad bridge in 1872. The population of Omaha in 1870 was 16,083. Twenty years later, after the growth spurred by the railroad, the population was 140,425. In the early days of transcontinental traffic, Omaha was thought of as the last civilized stop before the-less-than-civilized territories still further west.

In the American west the construction of the rail lines made it much easier for cattle ranchers to get their herds to the eastern markets. Major railroad stops were created, which became known as cattle towns, or cowtowns. For at least a few years, these newly-developed locations were usually extremely violent and lawless, and they contributed a major part of the lore and legend of what became known as "The Wild West."

Below: By the end of the nineteenth century, dining cars on rails both in Europe and North American could match the elegance—if not quite the grandeur—of the floating palace and luxury liners.

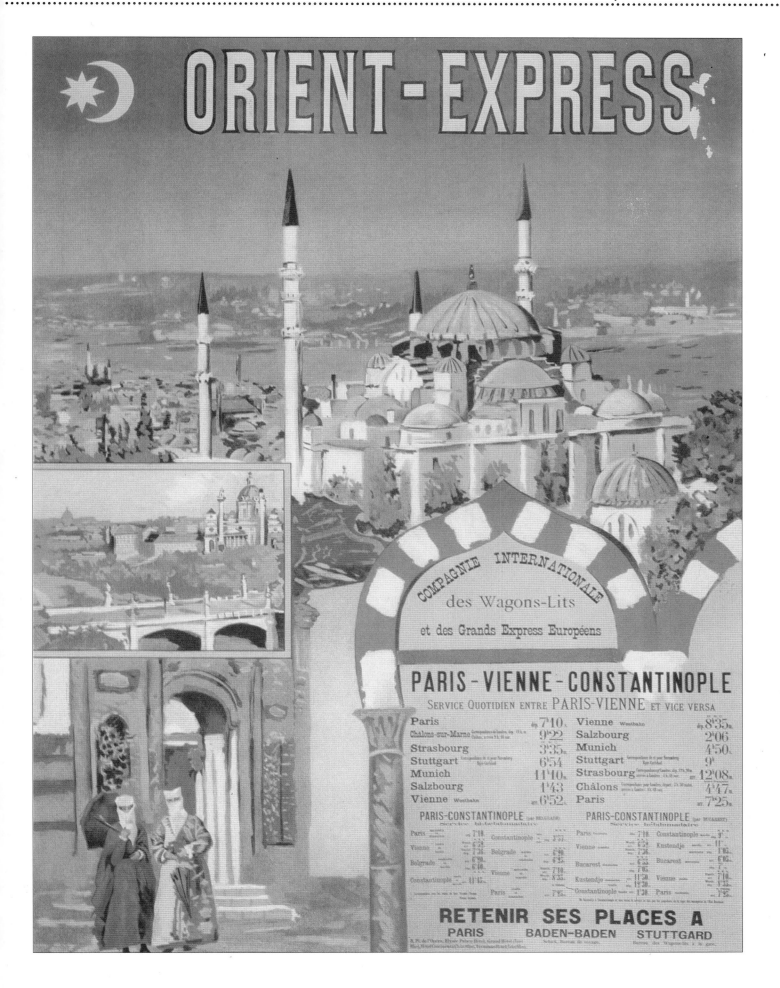

INDEX

Page numbers in **boldface** refer to picture captions.

Adlard, H., engraving by, **17**
Africa, steamers in, 6, **18**
Albany, New York, 12, **12**
Allen, Horatio, 54
America, 29
American Steamship Company, 27
Arctic, 38
Asian railroads, 69-70
Atlantic, 25, 38

Baltic, 38
Baltimore, 54, 64
Baltimore & Ohio Railroad, 54
Best Friend of Charleston, 54-57
Black Ball Line, 23
Blenkinsop, John, 51
Boston, 7, 9, **34**, 64
Britannia, 23, 38
Brunton, William, 51

Canada, 59, 64, 75
Canadian Pacific Railroad, 64, 75
Catlin, George, *St. Louis From the River Below*, 20
cattle towns (cowtowns), 78
Central Pacific Railroad, 59, **64**, 70-75
Chicago, 75-78, **77**
Chicago and Northwestern RR, 78
circus transport, **62**
Civil War steamers, 36, 39, 48
Clermont (*North River of Clermont*), 11, 12, **12**, 13
Cleveland, Ohio, 17
coal transport, **52**, 53
Collins Line, 25, 27, 38
Commonwealth, 48
Cooper, Peter, 7, 54
cotton transport, 20-22
Cugnot, Nicholas, 51
Cunard, Samuel, 23
Cunard Line, 6, 23, **25**, 27, 36-38
Cuneo, Terence, painting by, **55**
Currier & Ives lithographs, **22**, 59
  The Lightning Express Trains, 59
  The Mississippi in Time of War, 39
  Rounding the Bend, 5

Danna, 38
Delaware and Hudson Canal Company, 53, 54
Delaware River steamboat, 11
Destroyer, 48
Deutschland, 47
Dickens, Charles, 36-38
diesel power, 9, 36
Disaster of the Great Eastern: State of Her Grand Saloon during the Gale, **42**
Dressing for Dinner (Lloyd), **42**
Drew, Daniel, 60
Dudley, R., drawing by, **41**
Durant, Thomas, 59

Eagle, **14**
Eclipse, 47
Elise, **16**
Empress of Britain, 47
English (British) railroads, 6, **55**, 59, **69**, 72
  early steam locomotives, 51-53, **53**
  royal train, 5, **55**, 57
  stations, 57, 59, 64
  tunnels, 51, **54**, 55
English (British) steamers, 5-6, **11**, 17, 22, 23
  mail ship, **18**
  naval ships, 23, 48
  ocean liners, 43, 47
  tugboats, 33
  yacht, **27**
Erie, Pennsylvania, 17
Erie Canal, 17-19, 32
Erie Railroad, 59, 60
Erie Station, Hornellsville, New York, **59**
Eugenie, empress of France, **29**
Europe
  railroads, 6, 59, 68, **77**, 78
  steamers, 5, 6, **14**, **18**, 22
  train robberies, **71**
Evans, Oliver, 11, 51

Fisk, Jim, 60

Fitch, John, 11, 12
floating palaces, 5, 9, **29**, **37**, 43-49
Florida waterways, steamboats for, 30
  train wreck, **71**
freight transport, 6, 17, 27, 60, **62**
Fulton, Robert, 5, 11-13, **11**, **12**, **13**, 27, 29, 30, 51-53
Fulton, 38

Gould, Jay, 60
Grand Republic, 47
Grant, Ulysses S., 36
Great Eastern, The, **40**, **41**, **42**
Great Lakes, 5, 17-19
Great Western, 25

Hail and Farewell, **18**
Harrison, Benjamin, **69**
Hedley, William, 51
Henry, Edward Lamson, *The 9:45 Accommodation*, 68
High Flyer, **16**
Hindostan, **18**
H.M.S. Terrible, **23**
Hornellsville, New York, station, **59**
Hudson River at West Point (Starring), **34**
Hudson River steamers, 12, **12**, 13, **29**, **33**, **34**, 47
  Erie Canal link with Great Lakes, 17-19
  Fulton-Livingston monopoly, 13-17, 33

Illinois, 19, 60
Illinois Central RR, 78
immigrant travel, 6, 19-20, 64
India, 6, **18**, 59
international railroads, 68-69
Istanbul (Constantinople), 68, 78

Jacobsen, Antonio, portrait by, **29**
J. M. White, 48

Kilsby Tunnel, England, 51

La Grande Station, Los Angeles, 64
Leith, **18**
Lexington, **37**
Lightning Express Trains, The (Currier & Ives), 59
Lincoln, Abraham, 70
Liverpool, England, 22-23, **25**, 27
Liverpool & Manchester Railroad, 6, 53, 55
Livingston, Robert, 11, 12, 13, 29
Lloyd, W. W., *Dressing for Dinner*, **42**
Locomotion, **52**
Locomotion Number 1, 53
locomotives, *see* steam locomotives
London, 6, **14**, **16**, 64
London & Birmingham Railway, 51
London Engineer, 27
Long Island Sound, 48
Lusitania, 43

mail transport, **18**, 23, 27
Ma Roberts, **18**
Mary Powell, 47
Massachusetts, **34**
Melrose, Andrew, *New York from New Jersey*, 33
Memphis, Tennessee, 22, 75
Michigan Central RR, 78
Midland Railway Morning Scotch Express, **72**
Mississippi in Time of War, The (Currier & Ives), 39
Mississippi River steamboats, **20**, 20-22, 29-30, 31-32
  floating palaces, 5, **37**, 47-48
  races, 38, 48-49
Missouri River steamboats, 30-31
Monjo, H., painting by, **48**
Morgan, J. P., 27
Murdoch, William, 51
Murray, Matthew, 51

Natchez, 48-49
New Orleans, **29**
New Orleans, 20, **20**, 22, **22**, 31, 48-49, 75
"New Way of Traveling by Steam" (cartoon), **16**
New York City, 7, 9, 12, **12**, 25, 27, **31**, **34**, 64
New York from New Jersey (Melrose), 33

New York State, 12, 13, 17, 29, 57
9:45 Accommodation, The (Henry), 68

Ocean Captain Combes the Elder (Roux), 6
ocean steamers, 6, **40**, **41**, **42**, 43, 47
  with masts and sails, **19**, 39, 43
  transatlantic, 6, 22-27, **25**, 33, 36-43
Ocean Steam Navigation Company, 23
Orient Express, 68, 77, **78**
Oructor Amphibolus, 51

Pacific, 38
Pacific Railroad Act (1862), 70
Paris, **16**, 68, 78
Park Square Station, Boston, 64
Pennsylvania Railroad Company, 27
Persac, A., painting by, **37**
Phoenix, 13
Pilgrim, 48
Pittsburg Landing, Tennessee, 36
Price, Bruce, 64
Priscilla, 9, 48
Providence, Rhode Island, **34**, 64
Puritan, 48

raft steamers, 36
railroads
  in England, 5, 6, 51-53, **51**, **54**, **55**, 57, 59, **59**, **72**
  in Europe, 6, 59, 68, 77, 78
  founder of, 5
  importance of, 5
  romance of, 75, 77
  steamboat travel superseded by, 7, 9, 49, 60
  and steamship transport, 27
  tunnels, 51, **54**, 55
  in the United States, 6-7, 27, 53-60, 59, 64, 70-78, 77
  into wilderness, 68-75, **72**
  railroad stations, 57, **59**, 61-64, 68, 78
  railroad towns, 75-78
Reading Doubleheader, 75
Richardson, Henry Hobson, 64
Richmond, 48
Riou, Edouard, painting by, **29**
robber barons, 59-60
Robbins Brothers Circus, **62**
Robert E. Lee, 48-49
Rocket, 53, **53**
Rounding the Bend (Currier & Ives), 5
Roux, Antoine, *Ocean Captain Combes the Elder*, 6
Rumsey, James, 11
Russia, 69

St. Louis, 43
St. Louis, 20, **20**, 47, 48, 49, 75
St. Louis From the River Below (Catlin), 20
St. Paul, 43
Santiago, Cuba, Battle of, **48**
Savannah, 22-23, **25**
Sebron, Hippolyte, painting by, **31**
Seven Oaks Tunnel, England, 54
Shreve, Henry, 31
Siam, **72**
Siberia, 69-70
South Carolina Railroad, 7, 54
Sovereign, 48
Spanish American War, 48
S.S. America, 29
Starring, Olivia C., *Hudson River at West Point*, **34**
steamboats and steamships
  competition from steam locomotives, 7, 9, 49, 60
  dangers of, **16**, **37**, **42**
  European, 5, 6, 6, **16**, **18**, 22, 43, 47
  floating palaces, 5, 9, **29**, **37**, 43-49, 78
  freight transport, 6, 17, 27
  Fulton's, 5, 11, **12**, 12-13, 51
  history of, 5-6, 7-9, 11-27
  labor aboard, 40
  layout and inner workings, **19**, **41**, 43
  leisure travel, 27
  races, 38, 48-49
  stern-wheeler and inland designs, 29-32
  tugboats, 32-36, **34**, 40
steam engines
  coal vs. wood-fueled, 60
  "compound," for tugboats, 36
  early land vehicles, 51

on early steamboats, 11, 12
for Mississippi steamboats, 31
multiple, on trains, 75
superseded by diesel and electric power, 9, 36
steamer landings, 20-22
steam locomotives, 7, 51-78, **52**, **60**, **72**
  American, 54-57, 59
  freight transport, **52**
  history of, 6, 7, 51-59
  location of fuel source, 51
  Rocket, 53, **53**
  steamboats superseded by, 7, 9, 49, 60
  Stephensons', 51-54, **53**
  superseded by diesels, 9
  Tom Thumb, 7
steam packets, **14**, 22, 33
steam rafting, 36
steam tugboats, 32-36, **34**, 40
Stephenson, George, 6, 51, **53**, 55
Stephenson, Robert, 51, 53, **53**
stern-wheelers, 29-32
Stevens, John, 13, 54
Stockton & Darlington Railway, 6, 53, 55
Stourbridge Lion, 54
Suez Canal, 29
Symington, William, 11

Thornton, 11
Titanic, 43
Tom Thumb, 7, 54
train robberies, **71**
trains, 9, 48
  dining cars, 78
  family scene aboard, **69**
  as literary and artistic locale, 70
  with more than one engine, 75
  passenger cars, 68
  presidential, **69**
  royal, 5, **55**, 57
train stations, 61-64, 78
train wrecks, **71**
transatlantic cable, **41**
transatlantic ocean liners, 6, 22-27, **25**, 33, 36-43
Trans-Caspian (Central Asiatic) railroad, 69
transcontinental railroads, North American, 64, 70-75, 78
Trans-Siberian Railroad, 69-70
trestle bridges, 77
Trevithick, Richard, 51
tugboats, 32-36, **34**

Union Depot, Providence, 64
Union Pacific Railroad, 59, **64**, **72**, 75
Union Station, New Haven, 64
United States, 23
United States railroads, 6-7, 53-60
  for coal transport, 53-54
  construction of, 6-7, **64**, 70-75
  early steam locomotives, 7, 53-57
  first passenger train, 7, 54
  robber baron era, 59-60
  standardization of rail sizes, 60
  stations, 64
  and steamship transport, 27
  towns along, 75-78
  transcontinental, **64**, 70-75
  trestle bridges, 77
  in the west, **64**, 75
United States steamers, 5, 6, 7-9, **31**
  floating palaces, 5, 9, **29**, **37**, 43-49
  major landings, **20**, 20-22
  and rail transport, 27
  river transport, 11-22, **13**, **20**, 29-32; tugboats, 32-36
  transatlantic liners, 23-27, **25**, 38-43

Vanderbilt, Cornelius, 60
Victoria, queen of England, 5, **55**, 57

Walters, S., lithograph by, **25**
Washington, 31-32
Waterloo Station, London, 64
Watt, James, 12
Western Metropolis, 39
White Star Line, 27
Windsor Station, Montreal, 64

York Station, England, 59

Zambezi River steamer, **18**